You're The Investor!

Email: wealthfuladventures@gmail.com

ISBN 978-1-7347526-1-8

When you spend money to make money, you're an investor!

You can invest in another business.

You can invest in your own.

Fruit Stand

You can invest in real estate and create happy homes.

You can purchase from your favorite company's shop.

Or own a piece of it when you invest in their stocks.

Be wise when investing, funds may rise but they can drop!

Be sure to explore!

These aren't the only investments you can do.

The most important investment you can make is an investment in YOU!

Invest in your knowledge, never stop learning.

Use financial lessons and you'll start earning!

Invest in your mind, invest in your health.

Money isn't the only form of wealth.

Now say it with me,

"The best investment is an investment in myself!"

GAMES AND

ACTIVITIES

WORD SEARCH

Business
Explore
Funds
Growth
Investor
Real Estate
Stocks

X	N	S	Z	E	X	P	L	O	R	E	K	M	Q	A
X	E	C	V	U	C	O	O	F	P	K	U	H	I	Z
M	N	T	O	K	D	G	I	X	U	R	Y	P	I	E
H	W	A	J	M	C	E	W	N	L	N	Y	B	G	X
L	K	C	M	H	G	Z	V	H	V	M	D	X	A	B
X	F	M	R	K	Y	S	D	B	R	E	V	S	J	A
Y	T	V	E	X	X	K	A	Y	P	L	S	P	S	A
O	D	D	A	O	M	D	H	Y	C	O	D	T	T	F
J	Y	G	L	G	R	O	W	T	H	A	C	Z	O	A
E	T	G	E	B	U	S	I	N	E	S	S	L	C	R
N	W	N	S	F	L	P	Y	J	W	E	L	W	K	S
C	P	A	T	J	P	N	A	Y	M	A	U	C	S	O
M	E	Z	A	L	L	H	B	P	J	E	M	X	B	X
D	Z	X	T	K	W	I	M	F	O	I	P	W	W	S
J	R	D	E	L	Z	L	G	T	W	G	Y	G	F	C

CROSSWORD PUZZLE

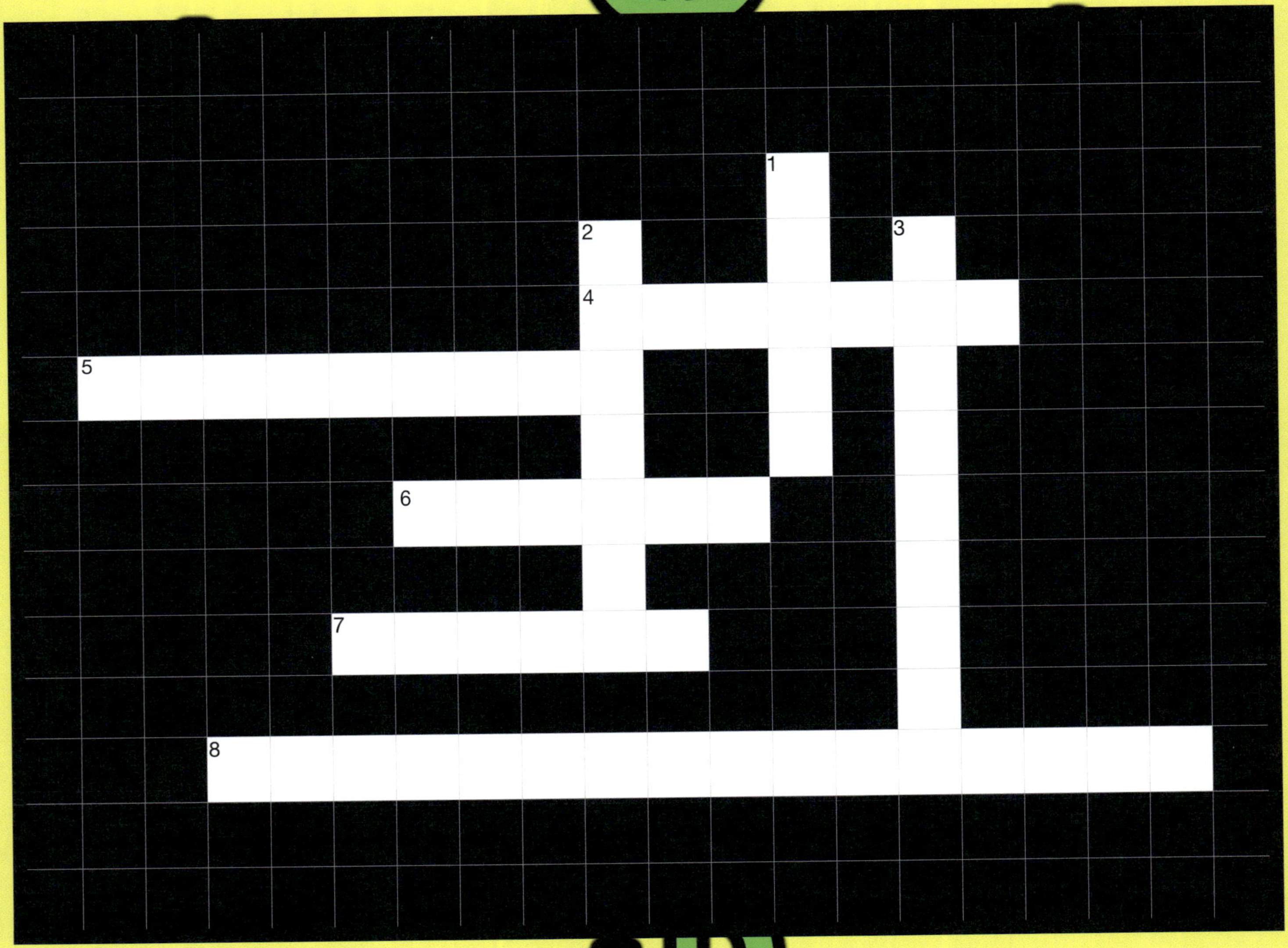

CLUES

Across

4 Making money.

5 Well-being, joy, or fulfillment.

6 Spending money to make more money.

7 Sustainable riches, health, knowledge, and peace.

8 When passive income is more than expenses.

Down

1 Currency used to make purchases.

2 Treating others kindly and accepting them as they are.

3 What you've learned.

WORD BANK

Earning
Financial Freedom
Happiness
Invest
Knowledge
Money
Respect
Wealth

FILL IN THE BLANK

1) When you spend ______ to make money, you're an __________!

2) You can invoke in __________ and create happy _______.

3) Be wise when investing, funds may _______ but they can _______!

4) Money______ the only form of ________.

5) The best __________ is an investment in __________!

Drop
Homes
Investment
Investor
Isn't

Money
Myself
Real Estate
Rise
Wealth

LIST WAYS TO INVEST

WORD SEARCH ANSWER KEY

X	N	S	Z	E	X	P	L	O	R	E	K	M	Q	A
X	E	C	V	U	C	O	O	F	P	K	U	H	I	Z
M	N	T	O	K	D	G	I	X	U	R	Y	P	I	E
H	W	A	J	M	C	E	W	N	L	N	Y	B	G	X
L	K	C	M	H	G	Z	V	H	V	M	D	X	A	B
X	F	M	R	K	Y	S	D	B	R	E	V	S	J	A
Y	T	V	E	X	X	K	A	Y	P	L	S	P	S	A
O	D	D	A	O	M	D	H	Y	C	O	D	T	T	F
J	Y	G	L	G	R	O	W	T	H	A	C	Z	O	A
E	T	G	E	B	U	S	I	N	E	S	S	L	C	R
N	W	N	S	F	L	P	Y	J	W	E	L	W	K	S
C	P	A	T	J	P	N	A	Y	M	A	U	C	S	O
M	E	Z	A	L	L	H	B	P	J	E	M	X	B	X
D	Z	X	T	K	W	I	M	F	O	I	P	W	W	S
J	R	D	E	L	Z	L	G	T	W	G	Y	G	F	C

CROSSWORD PUZZLE ANSWER KEY

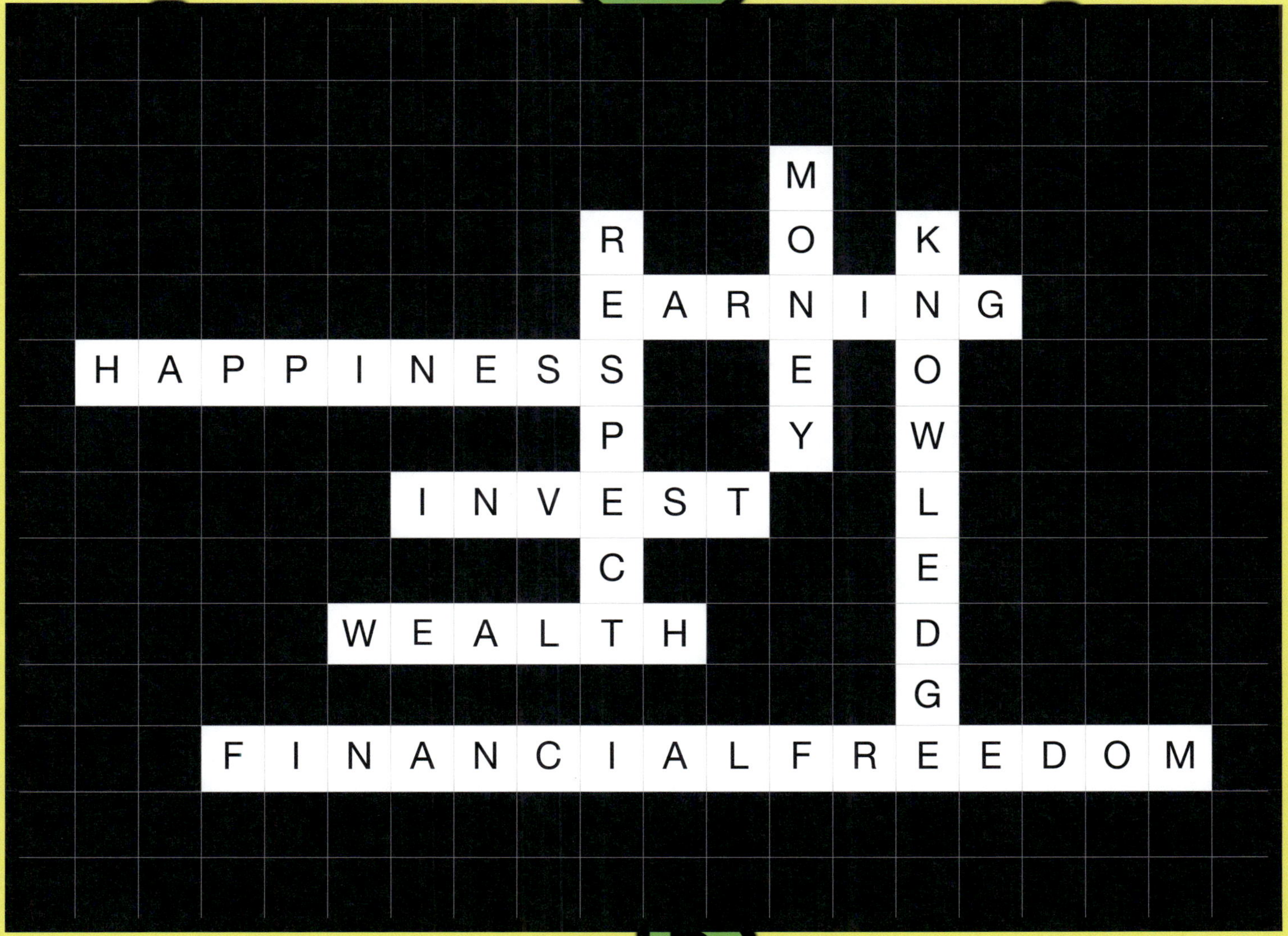

GLOSSARY

Business: A company or trade used to make money.

Financial Lessons: Learning how to manage money.

Financially Free: When passive income is more than expenses.

Funds: Money.

Invest: Spending money to make more money.

Passive Income: Money made with little to no effort.

Purchase: Buy a product.

Real Estate: Buildings or land.

Stocks: A piece of ownership in a company.

Wealth: Sustainable riches, health, knowledge, and peace.

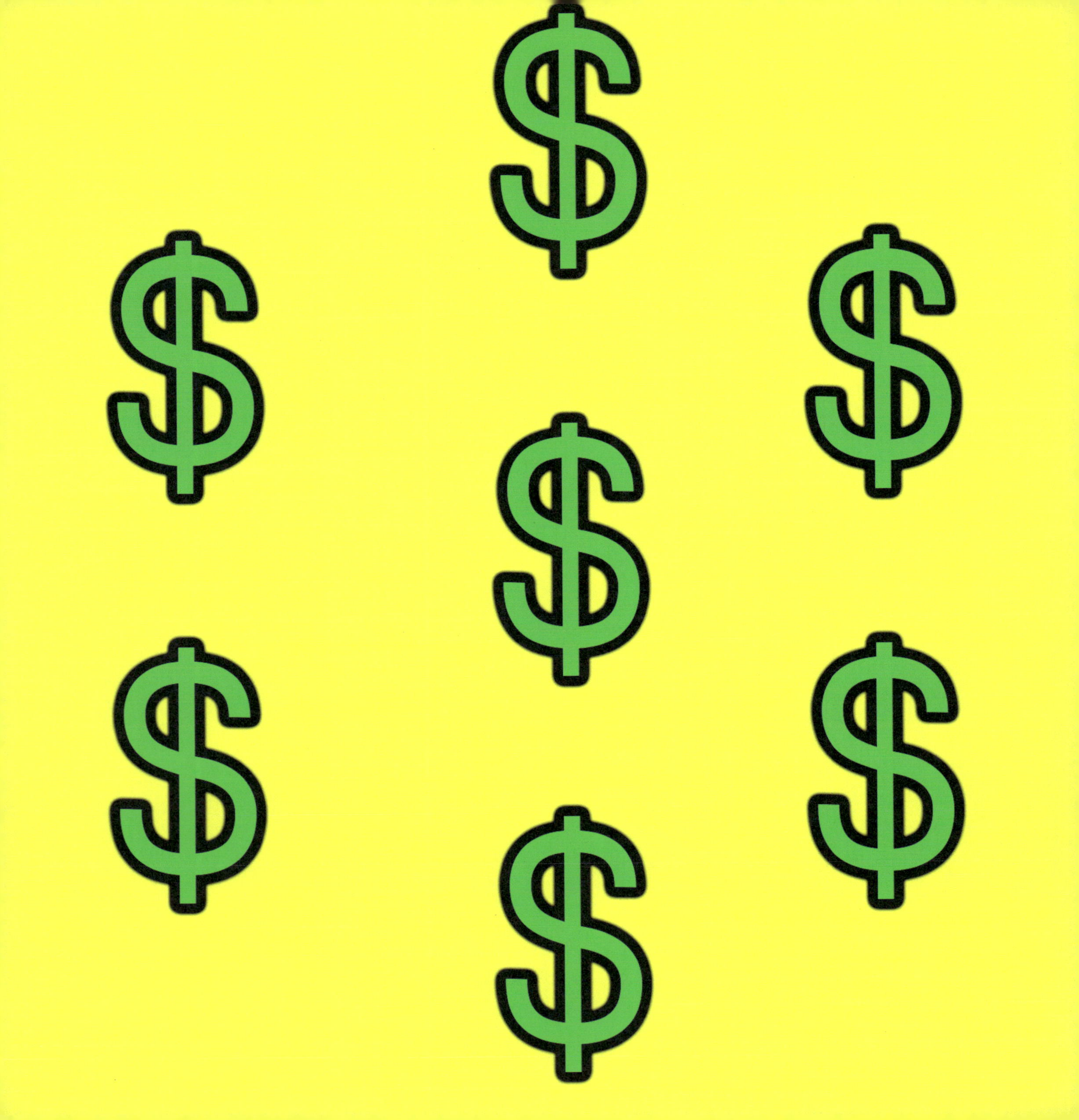

With repetition, these concepts can be grasped by the youngest readers. Please don't underestimate children's intelligence.

Made in the USA
Las Vegas, NV
07 November 2026

57672510R00019